Universe

Universal Rentboy

Chloe Poems

the bad press

Published in 2000 by
The Bad Press,
PO Box 76, M21 8HJ
www.thebadpress.com

ISBN 1 903160 04 9

All rights reserved.
Copyright Chloe Poems 2000.
A CIP catalogue record for this book
is available from The British Library.

1 3 5 7 9 2 4 6 8

Introduction copyright
The Divine David.
Cover designed by Robert Cochrane.
All photographs of Chloe Poems
by Hayley Slater-Ling.
Chloe as a child
by Gary Parkinson.

Printed by
The Arc & Throstle Press Limited
Nanholme Mill, Shaw Wood Road,
Todmorden, Lancs, OL14 6DA.

Distributed by
Turnaround
27 Horsell Road,
London N5 1XL.

Contents

Universal Rentboy I	09
Show-Business Is A Cancer And It's Riddled With Disease	10
Mirrorballin'	11
Manchester Queen, Glittery Top	14
Liverpool Queen, Bad Trip	18
London Is Paranoid	21
Some Of My Best Friends Are Straight	25
In Celebration Of Poo	27
The Queen Sucks Nazi Cock	30
Licking Prince Charles' Arse	33
Crash! Bang! Wallop! What a Picture!	36
Skinny Wee Dalek	39
Never Trust A Fella Whose Legs Are Too Close Together	42
Mind The Gap	45
Gothic	49
Blood On Satan's Boyfriend	53
Vegetarian Vampire Of Old Dudley Town	55
Kinky Boy	57
Drag Is Dead	59
It's Almost As If Hitler Won	61
I've Got Hair	64
Billy, Don't Be A Hairdresser	67
Faith Is A Toilet	70
I Wanna Be Fucked By Jesus	71
I Wanna Be Fucked By Jesus Too	74
All God's Children	75
We Travel	78
My Effeminate Bottom	81
I Don't Have A Cunt	83
Spud-u-Like In Monochrome	85
Universal Rentboy II	87
Gingham Footnotes	88

Dear Comrades

I'm Chloe Poems, and I'm a poet. I'm happy to tell you 'poet', as I don't feel I have to stress 'transvestite'. But some of you may want me to... Very well, I'm Chloe Poems and I'm a transvestite. A gay transvestite. A gay Socialist transvestite. A gay Socialist transvestite poet. And that's as close to compromise as I get.

"Compromise, compromise is no great agenda.
Compromise, compromise is frilly surrender.
So from the stick on my lips
To my hand-woven gingham suspender,
Ain't no compromise from this gender bender."

Welcome to this, my first collection of lovely poetry, 'Universal Rentboy'. "And why 'Universal Rentboy'?" I telepathically hear you ask. Well, we've all got something to sell. For some, it's the corporate mass packaging of stilted identity, corny smiles and hamburgers with relish - the rank canker that is capitalist consumerism.

But for others, like myself, it is hopefully the emancipation of the spiritual, physical and political soul; a plane of thought which both envelops and releases you, the real you. My sincerest wish is that this collection goes some way in achieving that.

So peruse at your leisure and pleasure. Share them with a friend, recite them at parties, W.I.s, or perhaps, at your local place of worship, eg, churches or toilets, they're all the same to me. Be loud about this book, for it has plenty to shout about. I embrace the spark of life that is all humanity's and wish you health, happiness, healing and revolution.

Gingham heals,
Comrade Poems.

p.s. The revolution will not be intellectualised.

Forewords & Backwards

"The horizontal and the vertical meet in liquid lines of language.

Miss Chloe Poems has been a compatriot of mine for a number of years now, and has a lot to bear in her basket, which she delivers to you fragrantly and flagrantly ... almost to your door.

Hoping your door is open, either way Miss Chloe "you bitch" Poems is a back-door kicker of international repute, whose verse has both quelled and insighted revolution globally.

It is well known that the spawn of ten-a-penny German princelings quake at the idea that Miss Chloe's poems will be etched and chiselled into the cold as stone facade that is Fucking'em Palace!

This People's Poet Laureate lives and breathes her work. Let her caress you like a delicate breeze about to become Tsunami.

This selection will become standard text in schools and encourage free expression in our kinder. Replacing 'Top of the Pops.'

All Hail Chloe Poems.
Hail Chloe.
Hail her vision.
Book now for the inevitable stadium sized gigs.
It's that simple.

Viva Free Verse!
To Nasturtium everywhere.

Chloe uber alles."

The Divine David

Dedication

I've been fortunate enough to have been surrounded by love
all my life. This book is dedicated to all those people
and girly sisters of all genders to whom I have said 'I love you';
to the energy that is life and love and especially to the energies
that were May Butler and Brian King
and is Betty.

Universal Rentboy (I)

Homosexuals used to scare me
and I would scream and shout
until I found homosexuals
left a lovely taste in the mouth.

Show-Business Is A Cancer And It's Riddled With Disease
Respectfully dedicated to the memory of Lena Zavaroni

Show-business is a cancer and it's riddled with disease
Show-business is a cancer and it's riddled with disease
Show-business is a cancer, Lionel Blair's dancer
Tony Blair's Prime Minister
Show-business is a cancer and it's riddled with disease.

Mirrorballin'

I'm coming up
I'm getting high
My hands are mimicking my mind
shadow puppeting pictures of such precise colour
silhouetting so many different things
all shapes and sizes
patterns uncompromising
rushes still rising
I'm capsizing and swimming right to the top.
Coming up too quickly
getting the bends
the pictures my mind sends
are pressurising me
contracting, refracting and contradicting my eyes
there's a world inside
and it wants to get out
a world inside
that wants to shoot out
star shaped clusters
open the shutters
my head's about to go supanova
Oh my God, I might fall over.
Must close my eyes and count to ten
one, three, seven, two
Jesus Christ there goes my head again.

I focus on a mirrorball
it gives me some position
like the North star to a sailor
Distressed, I send a signal
I rocket and flare

the mirrorball smashes everywhere
trashes round the dance floor
a million shards and more
each reflecting a piece of me.

Wow, I'm Mirrorballin' babe
ain't no stallin'
I'm past controllin'
as I'm freefallin'
into love so ecstatic
It's prismatic
The world around me
is a spirallin' scene of funfair magnitude
Fuck attitude
cos I'm Mirrorballin' babe
rollercoastin'
boastin' about my new found mind as the old one lumbers
I don't believe it
I think I can see the lottery numbers
must write them down
but now I'm being bounced around.

Wow, I'm Mirrorballin' babe
my finger's on the trigger and I'm gonna pull it
I'm pinballin' babe
a shooting sphere of steel faster than a speedin' bullet
ricochetin' displayin' and paradin' my fantasy
Tilt!
It's incredible
this is so cerebral
almost unbelievable

slowing down then suddenly rushed
poor old Humpty Dumpty
did he fall or was he pushed?

I'm mirrorballin' babe
metamorphin' into shapes and sizes I've never been
It's a wonderland of the divine and the obscene
I choose an image then I grab it
and there's Richard Gere as Alice
being fist fucked by a white rabbit.

I'm Mirrorballin' babe
and coming through a whirlwind of gargantuan proportions
Hey Mister, it was a twister
resplendent in all its contortions
it's taken me over the hill
and back into my minds eye.
For some reason somewhere
I don't know why
I'm standing perfectly still
Beautifully lit
whispering
"I'm ready for my close-up Mr DeMille."

I'm Mirrorballin' babe
Mirrorballin'
Mirrorballin' babe
Mirrorballin'
Mirrorballin' babe
Mirrorballin'.

Manchester Queen, Glittery Top

On the dance floor
in the club
boppin' to Kylie
well I'm that kind of gay
I'm all a jitter
in this disco glitter
and I ain't got much to say.
Dancin's kinda clumsy
hips kinda bumpy
confidence is draining away
Ooer, Kylie's reached a high
Shit, so must I
but there's only one way.
Wait for me Kylie
not just yet
let me get them to my nose.
I'm shocked by the power
every single hour
Fuckin' hell, here it goes

Nothing's gonna stop us
sniffin' our poppers
Nothing's gonna stop us now
Gosh, it's great
this amyl nitrate
Betcha by golly
Wow

Coming down
what a whoosh
Kylie would be proud

It took all the strength I mustered
now I'm kinda flustered
just like the rest of the crowd
Kylie's gone and faded
everyone looks jaded
what are we gonna do next?
Ooh, there's someone I fancy
he doesn't look too nancy
and he's wearing one of those fabulous
L'Homme Clone Zone vests.

Madonna's on now
and he's coming over
his moustache makes me weak.
He asks me my name
and then for a sniff
and I can hardly speak.
Madonna's near the chorus
it's like she's doing it for us
Hold on Madonna
don't be shoddy
I take out my poppers
we sniff real hard
Oh erotic, erotic!
Put your hands all over my body.

Nothing's gonna stop us
sniffin' our poppers
Nothing's gonna stop us now
Gosh, it's great
this amyl nitrate
Betcha by golly
Wow

His tongue's down my throat
my head's on the moon
his hands are inside my Calvin Klein's
I start to come too
he whispers "I wanna fuck you,"
not the most romantic of chat-up lines.
We leave the club
I hail a cab
I try to talk to him politely
but he's not interested in chat
and the reason is that
he's trying to stick his fingers up my bum in the taxi.

He gets me home
and into bed
ever so slyly he slips on Kylie
and says "what do I have to do to get it through to you
you horny little bitch"
I say "You red hot stud
I'll chew your cud
but there's just one hitch
I dropped my poppers in the club
and without them I can't take it up my botty".
He nods, smiles, gives a knowing look
that says "hey kid, don't you worry"
He opens the door to his bedside cabinet
and much to my surprise
a thousand bottles come pouring out
it was a popper pickin' sniffin'
Kylie smiley fuckin' paradise

Nothing's gonna stop us
sniffin' our poppers
Nothing's gonna stop us now
Gosh it's great
this amyl nitrate
Betcha by golly
everything's jolly
Betcha by golly
WOW!

Liverpool Queen, Bad Trip

Oh no, What am I like
I've took too many trips
me tongue feels huge
the club's like jelly
and me fingers look like chips
chips from the Chippy, not French Fries
me eyes look like French Fries
no surprise really.
Ooh, this is getting really scary
now me tongue feels as hairy
as Tom Selleck's chest.
Is this some kind of test?
I feel null and void
"Fuck off will you mate.
I'm not getting paranoid"

That Manchester Queen in the glittery top
is looking at me strange
like I'm deranged
me brain feels like size twelve feet in Kate Moss's shoes
what's worse
I really, really need a poo
Shit, what am I gonna do
Me arse feels like there's a turtle's head
popping out its shell
Now I'm starting to feel sickly
best I find a toilet quickly
Fuckin' twattin' shittin' hell
me head's destroyed
"Fuck off will you gays
I'm not getting paranoid"

The club's the size of Sydney
just as fucking busy
and the bog's the other side
I cut through the crowd
and hope I can be seen
but everyone's the size
of wibbly wobbly jumping beans.
Oh no, I'm drowning in a sea of moustaches and leather
some of the fellas look like ladies
they're all turning into drag queeny jelly babies
and I'm at the end of me fuckin' tether
I scream at the top of me voice
"Will somebody show me the toilet!
I'm starting to get annoyed"
a finger points to a door in the distance
I say "Thank you very much
and I'm not getting fuckin' paranoid!"

I run as fast as I can
me legs are like elastic bands
a twingin' and a twangin' across the disco floor
I've never wanted a shit more

I rush to the door that was pointed out
somebody shouts "It's pitch black in there"
but I don't care
I drop me 501's as quick as I dare
let out the biggest blast of farty air
and a dump the size of Tenerife
Oh what a relief!
A smile spreads across my face
as the smell cuts the gloom

A voice says
"Thankyou very much I needed that"
I start to feel a prat
as I realise
I'm in the fuckin' dark room.
The bloke starts a chatting
"I'm really into scatting"
I feel less than overjoyed
why did it have to happen
I wish I was in Prestatyn
'cos now, now
Now I'm really fucking paranoid!

London Is Paranoid

London is Paranoid
a hapless void
of polarised pretension
of anal retention
an invention
of media, money and power.
London is sour
a dour metropolis
ruined as the Acropolis
hanging on a precipice
of insufficient power
an imposing edifice
rocking, rotting
second by minute
minute by hour
into the murky waters
of a disenfranchised river
I watch it wither
I see it quiver
with fear
limp, lame and sore
always looking over
it's own cold shoulder
that it overlooked before.
That's not because it's caring
it just wants to check out
what you're wearing

London is Paranoid
a place enjoyed
by the rancid cancer
of celebrity

I say "Let it be"
it wants to be A List
so happy to be B List
and if not I'll see you on the C List
but please God,
never on the D
and these showbiz cadavers
call this credibility

So magazine
So limousine
Has Been
And Maybelline
If you're skin's not tangerine
then you're yesterday's news
I'm sorry mate
you're second rate
if you don't live in
a Mews.

London is Paranoid
far more destroyed
by its attitude
than it ever was in the blitz
it's in bits
Bitchin' and snitchin'
Scritchin' and scratchin'
each others eyes out
and these personality clashes
haven't ruined just eyelashes
they've left yawning gaping gashes
in its soul
so tawdry and cold.

It's a catalyst
dreamt up by a Capitalist
who claimed it's streets
were paved with gold
Fools Gold
so turn again
bid it Hasta Manana
for London is the epicentre
of Cruel Britannia.

London is Paranoid
shop soiled
and unemployed
left to fester
in its own celebration
its head hung
in a noose
of facile elation
but give a city enough rope
and it will hang a nation
starved of emotional nourishment.
Now that's what I call
Capital Punishment.

London is creeping
dripping, seeping
into the consciousness
of us all
we can all fall under its spell
London is hell
where the concepts of humanism
are engulfed by the flames of consumerism
so watch out
for you might get caught.

So please remember
you must remember
that you, you, you and you
you're much more important
than the last thing you bought.

London is paranoid.

Some Of My Best Friends Are Straight

When I'm out clubbing
I love to shake my bootie
I'm hot stuff in hot pants
a gingham groove thang.
All the gay boys
they think me a cutey
a disco explosion
a jolly good bang.
But not just the gay boys it seems
to my straight friends
I'm the life and soul of the party
a vision of loveliness
a poly-cotton dream
why I'm often taken to the toilet
to do a line of Charlie
but coke does strange things to a straight man
If you know what I mean.
"'Ere Chloe, the Charlie's made me horny
cop a load of this
but don't tell John, Pete and Nige"
I say "Don't be silly Alfredo
I know the story morning glory"
but what he doesn't know is
John, Pete and Nige
have already been more than happy to oblige.
And with my mouth full
and Alfredo off his tits
I think "Omni, Omni, Omni, Suck, Suck, Lick
Isn't it great
that some of my best friends are straight?"

Oh how I love playing football
with the rest of the lads
we're a real hard hitting, ball kicking, beer swilling
Sunday League team
but some of those boys really are cads
because they're straight acting, non scene
Sunday League queens.
On the field I may be the only left winger
but I'm not the only one
who's a little bit ginger.
I love it on the pitch
displaying our masculine powers
but believe me
there's a lot more dribbling
going on in the showers.
When I handle a ball
it's never a foul
but it all depends on the ball I pick
and if I'm sent off
it's usually with Harry
now that's how I get my free kick
and Harry always says
"I've never done this before
you won't tell the others will you mate"
and I reply
"Omni, Omni, Omni, Suck, Suck, Lick
isn't it great
that some of my best friends are straight?"

In Celebration Of Poo

What a wonderful thing Poo is
It comes in many wondrous shades of brown
It's so fulfilling squeezing it out
especially when you're sitting down
flicking through your Vanity Fair
smiling contently
not giving a care.
Why, sometimes it's even as brown
as Demi Moore's hair
What a wonderful thing Poo is!

What a wise thing Poo is
living contently
snuggled in our colon
pondering interplanetary toilet seats
especially when it's on one
zooming around in interstellar loos
touching on universal truths
it screams out excitedly
Ureka, This is It!
how can we love ourselves
if we can't love our shit!
What a wise thing Poo is.

What a sexy thing Poo is
with its dusky allure
and provocative perfume
Poo, sexy?
you're looking at me like you're not sure
what else do grown men get up to
in the Little Boys' Room

they're not just there for the culture
they're not just there for the soul
they're there to stick their willies
through next doors glory-hole
What a sexy thing Poo is.

Poo! Poo!
You do, I do
so why then do some of us pretend not to
If we deny our natural bodily endeavour
then naturally
we'll be crippled for ever and ever
so open your arse
let your bowels be free
it's time to celebrate
our poo and wee.
Let our powers be demonstrated
no longer will we be constipated
it's time our poo was elevated
to its highest state.
Why, I bet even the Virgin Mary and the Baby Jesus
just love a good poo
inside those Pearly Gates.

What a profound thing Poo is
Let's acknowledge it's effect on ourselves.
It's no mystery
we've poo'd through history
I can't believe it's the year 2000 and we're still not used to
pooey smells
don't turn your nose up
open your mind
why be afraid to find
that you're a rectal thinker

be like me
spit on your finger
and probe the soft, moist joys
of your fascinating sphincter.
As the old saying goes
Poo does, as Poo knows
What a profound thing Poo is!

The Queen Sucks Nazi Cock

How I adore
the lush green amour
of my England.
No tower blocks roar
smoke does not pour
to pollute
my lush green England.
I salute my England
this subtle land
where whispering breezes
go hand in hand
with foxgloves
and the gentle down of
dandelion feather
the heather
pinks and purples
streams rhyme and gurgle
hares chase and hurdle
across her morning moist dewy fields.
The hills and valley yield tenderly
their softness and nobility.
I'm a million miles from cruelty
here in my lush green England
floating o'er moor and lake
impervious to trouble
it seemed nothing in this genteel land
could burst my idyllic bubble.

So you must understand my surprise
nay, my horror, my shock
when I found out that
the Queen sucks Nazi cock.

Yes, the Queen sucks Nazi cock.
Can you believe it
that someone so royal, so perfect
could do something so heinous?
Your Royal Heinous, Elizabeth
the bastion of majesty
orally caressing her husband's erectile racist penis
a right royal travesty
an unequivocal tragedy
of unimaginable proportions.

Does this also mean
my lush green England
is merely a series of such abhorrent distortions
sold as a package
to an over-eager, overseas market
who see our history
as nothing more
than rolling hills, the Rolling Stones
and rolling red carpet?

The Queen sucks Nazi cock.
When I came to terms with it
there could be no more denial
I stand
stranded a million miles away
observing this septic isle
saddened lonely
a solitary position
as my lush green England dissolves
into chaos and division
where an Englishman's castle
is the crumbling housing
on a drug-run council estate

where the elderly live in fear
relics of another age
twisted by grief and rage
bemused and broken
that they should be left
to such a fate
in this lush green police state.
My England is a series of hells
black bodies murdered
in prison cells,
a stark contrast
to the green hills and fells
we're force fed
as our staple diet
gorging on national identity.
I thought we were meant to be
free citizens of democracy
yet we sit content
and in judgement
to single out
single mothers
as society's ultimate heresy.
It seems we never stop burning witches
and this is England,
my England
where the blue bloodied Hanoverians
are the true blue barbarians
who rule o'er
this stagnation and rot
how could they not
when the head of the highest
family in all the land
our Mother Protector
Her Royal Heinous the Queen
sucks Nazi cock.

Licking Prince Charles' Arse

Who'd have thought it
Who'd have guessed
Was it all pretend?
Just what was it you meant by politics?
What causes were you really holding so close to your chest?
Was your anger facsimile?
Now this may come across suspiciously
but did you really care?
And just where was Thatch
Sorry, Mrs Thatcher
in all of this
Was she your enemy
or just a handy catchphrase
a right hook
with which to grab an audience.
Oh gloom, doom, despondency, despair
I naively thought you genuine
warriors in the class war
comedy guns blazing
targeting bureaucracy
someone to side with in those
extremely bleak
right wing years.
I foolishly believed your tissue of lies
so funny it sometimes hurt my sides
moved to tears of laughter
by those stories of the Glasgow shipyards,
I sensed your history profoundly
your witty banter would
enthral and astound me
it was almost as if you cared.

But the joke it appears was on us
an audience punch drunk with laughter
gullible enough to support
and roar out our approval
belly aching with recognition
each working class rendition of life
before the removal of your honour and integrity.
We were the ticket buying public
you allowed to buy into
your calculated treachery.

You've moved house now
you're on the other side of the street
how sweet
but to keep the audience stringing along
you've had to keep your accents strong
and your true politics undetectable
you've become acceptable,
even worse, integral in their arsenal
arseholes,
you're rubbing shoulders allows them
to look respectable
giving them that much needed common touch.
Can't you see what's going on?
Don't you understand?
you're nothing but dish-rags
cleaning the blood from off their hands.

The red flag don't fly no more
now you're red carpeting your way to the palace
how callous
you used to be flies in the ointment
now you're comedy by royal appointment
court jesters caught in the act of hypocrisy.

Tell me again
just what was alternative comedy?
Does it mean you're laughing all the way to the bank?
It was just a load of wank wasn't it?
How can you claim loyalty
parading around in this theatre of cruelty
when you've been caught well and truly
with your pants down?
Oops, there goes Her Majesty's knickers
then you bow
your head hung low
tongues so brown
cowering, drooling in front of the crown.
Don't you feel guilty
fooling around in this terrible farce?
You must feel ashamed
licking Prince Charles' arse.

Crash! Bang! Wallop! What A Picture!
(A brutal tribute to Princess Diana)

Crash! Bang! Wallop! what a picture!
Princess Pretty, porcelain precise
image concise on cup and saucer
marital bliss embittered
skin and bone shattered
a lifetime battered
into the twisted metal
that contorted the fairytale lovely
until she was splattered on more than
just our front pages.

The ages will suggest a saint
and paint a picture of selfless duty
wrapped in beauty
that comforts and heals.
Marian visions with tears for the poor,
the injured, the beguiled,
the unsure and bewildered
will gather where her memories lie
demanding love from beyond the grave.
Is this Saint Frankenstein
an unfortunate creature of our own making
lumbering clumsily through a soft-focused
rose-tinted insistence of England
so green and pleasant
or a graveyard where they still shoot pheasant.

Crash! Bang! Wallop! What a picture!
Limousine wealthy
Parisian couture
A woman more than human

a most significant other
even bigger than a mother
who captured the spirit of our sick and lonely.
Oh, such macabre poetry
if only she'd survived
it now seems the world was a much better place
when she was alive.
The sun shone more
rain wasn't acid
and the acrid stench of pollution was dissolved into
a commemorative bone china cup
of milk and honeysuckle.
How can we struggle on
now that our hope has gone?
Thank God we've still got Elton John.

Fashion icon, media whore
a seducer with the Midas touch
sometimes coy, often sultry
but would we have forgiven short squat Mother Theresa
if she'd committed adultery?
It's easy to create a Saint
when she's pretty.

Crash! Bang! Wallop! What a picture!
Saint Frankenstein you floored a nation
with your oh so dramatic exit.
History tells it so graphically
but mothers die every day
and without a principality
so what makes you so special?
But I somehow believe you cared
a woman flawed and unprepared
for the ravages of a media led society.

The very people who mourned you
are the same savages who mauled you
and hauled you through the tabloids
feeding off your trauma and anxiety.
Even in death there is no rest
we're still picking at your rotting flesh.
We're fighting back the crocodile tears
because we mustn't miss the souvenirs
a mug, a thimble, a vase or a plate.
We'll buy anything adorned with
Saint Frankenstein's face.

Lady Di
Lady dead
Lady buried
Laid to rest?
I hope we were mourning a woman of compassion
and not Princess Pretty and the death of fashion.

Skinny Wee Dalek

Doctor
I dinnae care if the Cybermen have got you
by the short and curlies
If I dinnae score soon Doctor, I'm sure to cold turkey.
Now I know you've got a problem with that
but I cannae find my biro
and if we dinnae land on earth soon
I'll no' be able to cash my giro.

Doctor
what d'ya mean there's a hole in the fabric
of space and time
and what's all this about being eaten by
an amorphous blob of green slime?
It's no' that I'm afeared
but I cannae find my biro
and if we dinnae land on earth soon
I'll no' be able to cash my giro.

Och, it seems that we have landed
and not a moment too soon
time and space travelling's lovely
but there's no' a post office up on the moon.
The Doctor's really nice
there's no-one kinder
saving the Universe is one thing
but there's no a decent needle exchange on Zeta Minor.

I'll no' be a minute Doctor
as I've just found my biro
and in just nine parsecs I'll have cashed my giro.

I dinnae believe that
I was standing in the queue
when this skinny wee Dalek said
"Sarah Jane McTucky, if you dinnae give me your giro
I'm gonna to exterminate you"
I said "Get to fuck, you skinny wee Dalek
I'm no getting taxed by a pepperpot
and if you dinnae get the first
matter transmitter out of here
I'm gonna tell your Mammy about your fiendish plot."
I told it to bog off
or I'd reverse the polarity of its neutron flow
'cos there was no way on this planet
it was getting its sucker on my hard earned giro.
I nutted it in the balls
all thirty-eight
I said "How's that for a Glasgae kiss,
you bubbling lump of hate?"
It trundled off with its blaster between its legs
and I screamed "You're lucky tae be alive"...
then I kind of felt sorry for it Doctor
'cos like me, it was just trying tae survive.

The galactic recession's hit
Universal domination really badly
and there's no' the opportunities there were
so I said "Hey, you, y' skinny wee Dalek,
d'ya fancy a lovely wee beer?"
Och, we got on really well
we had a lot in common
it was great at footbae in school
and when it played Batman, like me
it was always Robin.

When it was time to say goodbye
I slipped it a fiver
'cos after all Doctor
it wasnae all bad.
Och, it hardly seems fair
even the Daleks have an underclass.

Is it like this everywhere Doctor
or are there places you can go
where you dinnae get threatened by extermination
when you wannae cash your giro?

Never Trust A Fella Whose Legs Are Too Close Together
(dedicated to the memory of Stephen Milligan)

It's very sad the way Stephen died
turkey trussed, bulging eyed
satsuma placed in hogshead facsimilie
it seems Stephen's death
was quite simply futile
the cause of many a wry smile
from close friends and colleagues
cruel lips whispering
"He was wearing Peter Lilley's 'Pretty Polly's'."

It's very sad the way Stephen died
secret laced like Victorian boots
an elegant stockinged ankle
held prisoner in a three piece suit.
So from a bowler hat and knickers
to a junior whip's umbrella
please
never trust a fella
whose legs are too close together.

How can a junior minister
be so bloody sinister?
How could he administer his post
when his diabolical acts
proved for a fact
he'd be walking through walls
as a parliamentary ghost?

A coin is defined by its two sides
one heads, the other tails
they sit close together

inseparable forever
like Harrods and January Sales.
But there's another side to a coin
the thin elegant circumference
as essential as the other two
but ignored by you and you
it binds them both in life
and dictates what they do.

Now I can toss a coin
I can toss my hair
run through the streets
with my legs in the air
tickle nuns
steal their habits
from Mrs. Shilling's hats I can pull out rabbits
polish my nails
and buff my muff
I can do all that extravagant stuff
so come with me
enter my camp dance
l can liberate you from your restricting pants
but as sure as Polly James is Eric Heiffer
please
never trust a fella whose legs are too close together.

It's very sad the way Stephen died
and the fact he had to hide
his lovely wardrobe from the world.
He had suspenders many girls would have killed for
or at least asked to borrow
and for me, that's the greatest sorrow
because it can really make you ill
if you can't share your greatest skill.

Stephen had ill health he had to live in
a lonely bungalow of despair
a place tangled and bitty
like so much unwashed pubic hair.
Like the crazy pantomime dame
Stephen bungled, then he came.
So why be Buttons when you can be Cinderella
Please, never trust a fella whose legs are too close together.

It's very sad the way Stephen died
amidst all his wealth.
It's very sad the way Stephen died
because he couldn't trussed himself.

Mind The Gap

What kind of Father
abandons his son?
What kind of father
denies the pain of others?
For example the mothers
who bring his children to earth
the gap between Heaven and Hell.
Mind the Gap I said
take care
those children are unique
let them be incomplete
let them seek
their nooks and crannies
Godsons and nannies
claim your celebration
be demons dancing in honour of a demon
chant incantations of filth
drink obnoxious concoctions
sing verses of impurity
revel in obscurity
forgo forsaking, swill around
in the glorious debauchery
of your own making.
Who say this?
I do!
Who am I?
I'm what happens when God gets bored of forgiving you.

Shackled, manacled
more than manhandled
how can you pull together
when it's clear
you're poles apart.

Mind the gap, I said
your mishap
I was his happy advisory
the Machiavellian chap
a bad boy story
banished from Paradise
and all His glory holy
cast down
because I would not hide
my sin of pride.
Oh God, you were all heart
when you thought
my heart burning
in sacrificial heat
but the flames
a licking and lapping
at my feet
made me jig 'n' dance
I enjoyed the pain
so let the demon dance again.
Who say this?
I do!
Who am I?
I'm what happens when God gets bored of forgiving you.

Mind the gap
the gap between
Heaven and Hell
women and men
go tell
of your desires.
I offer you
the fires of invention
wear your sexual intention.

Fuck monogamy
swap your cocks and cunts
destroy convention
prepare your sodomy
and make no apologies
for your androgyny.

Mind the gap
The gap between
the wheres and whyfores
of wicked thoughts
and trickster hordes.
Oh bring on the dancing whores
and bicker
to the chaos and rhythm
tear down His pearly gates
break out of the prison.

Mind the gap
The gap between Heaven and Hell
the place where fallen angels dwell
in city, alley, wood and vale.
Give them voice to tell their tales
then let their voices run away
to tell their tales another day.

What kind of Father
demands you see no further than His narrow vision?
To always seek forgiving
the sins you can't avoid,
"Lest your soul be destroyed
in the raging fires of Hell".
Well, I bid you welcome my friend
bring your baggage and your toil

become embroiled in my feast
let's feast together
on wine and words, gorge
at least until our stomachs burst.
I promise it won't hurt
my promise I shall keep
and if you should fall into a rest so deep
no worries,
for nightmares are beautiful daydreams
where I sleep.
Who say this?
I do!
Who am I?
I'm what happens when God gets bored of forgiving you.

Gothic

We are a distant castle
film noir and night-kissed,
dimly lit by moonlight
silhouetted
a crumbling chateau
mist shrouded in silver.
Some consider this cold my love
to surround yourself
in the crumbling ruins
of yesteryear.

But they fear the dark
we welcome
and swallow with
open mouths, eyes, arms, heart.
They jump and start
at rat scuttling sounds
they're unable to envision.
Imprisoned by ignorance,
housed cosy small
in two up, two down security,
screaming despair
at walls they're too frail
to break through
in case passionless hearts attack
and leave limp, lifeless,
the minds and bodies
it already took a lifetime to ignore...

And they consider us
Undead, unalive
Shadowless

hollow beings
condemned to stalk
the dim, dark, dank corridors
of their restricted imagination.
They see us merely
as an analogy
of their own
infertility,
guilt, and inherent stagnation.

Oh, but our love is
Gothic
Overwhelming
Sprawling, splendid
A Grand Guignol
cathedral
with catacombs never ending,
the sonorous
sound of doom impending
echoing a symphony
intending
to soundtrack a film
James Whale
could be directing.

Our love is
Gothic
creatures of the night
blood soaked in passion
without responsibility.
We're vapour
riding moonbeams
formless
unrestricted by conformity.

A testimony
to poets
and storytellers
unafraid of
love's link to mythology.
We're music of the night
Pitched perfect and free
Pitched perfect and free
Pitched perfect and free.
Cutting, screaming
through the air.
Some might say, my love
ephemerally,
ethereally
but always eternally.

Our love is
Gothic
Bonded as damp
dripping down dungeon walls
We are waterfalls
liquid collecting
into the gutters and sewers
of lust and joy
exploring
unfettered sexuality
boy girl, girl boy
or any number of combinations.
We're a pendulum swinging
with no respect for time.
We're Madame Guillotine
about to tear into the
bottomless pit
of a gutless mankind

and display their entrails
victorious, strident, naked
wearing with satisfaction
only the most
Machiavellian of smiles
as a distant church chimes
witching hour
bewitching hour.
We're bats chirruping
in and out of the bell tower
the night chorus
peeling,
ringing out our song
we can do no wrong
our love is so strong
it will outstrip time
it's experimental
monumental
the highest point
of any temple,
our love is
Gothic.

Blood On Satan's Boyfriend

I was trolling through the graveyard
it must have been twelve o'clock
when I saw the most fearsome thing
it were the devil's cock
it were huge and stank of sulphur
I wondered where he came from
and when he turned around
He had the cutest Beelzebumbum
I screamed, but it weren't with fear
it were more with sheer delight
as the devil went and said to me
will you be my boy tonight.
He fucked me over gravestones
He flung me in the air
He dragged me round the graveyard
by my twinkie permed hair.
I had to grin and bear it
as I just couldn't stop him
and you would too
if you had the devil's balls
banging against your bottom.

Blood on Satan's boyfriend!

It were nine months later
on the sixth of the sixth, ninety-six
I was in a club, chatting up this bloke.
He asked me if I was into bondage
when Splash! my waters broke
I felt very embarrassed, then I apologised
and when I looked again
he had the devil's eyes.
I was rushed into the labour ward

I could still hear the devil's cackle.
The nurse said "push" and I pushed hard
then the doctor announced
I was the proud father of a bonny baby Jackal...
I cried as I told the nurse
that I would call him Arthur
he had the cutest devil's button nose, the softest devil's skin
he looked just like his father.
Then at the Christening
as we were wetting the baby's head
laser beams shot from his eyes
and all me mates dropped dead.

Blood on Satan's Boyfriend.

Well, I couldn't have him killing my friends
so I knew he must be stopped
then I read in an ancient book
that said, "off his head must be chopped".
As I raised my axe above his bonce
I shivered and went cold
how could I kill my poor little Arthur,
he was only three days old,
but this little boy was a monster
and I had to save the world
but I couldn't help thinking
how different things might have been
if my Arthur had been a girl.
I asked God to guide my hand
to make it strong, swift and true
then Splat! I severed his demonic wicked evil little head
and that was the end of my Arthur
Omen Two.

Blood On Satan's Boyfriend.

Vegetarian Vampire Of Old Dudley Town

It's not easy being the only vegetarian vampire
of old Dudley town
you don't half look stupid in front of your mates
Dracula won't hang round with me any more
and Vlad the Impaler has taken to asking Nosferatu out
whenever he gets a couple of virgins on a double date.
I'm kind of left on me tod really
but I don't mind, 'cos I've got me principles
and I'm sticking to them like glue
but it would be nice just for a change
to change into a bat and fly around the moon,
y'know, like we used to do.
But oh, no, not any more
They're too busy aren't they
terrorising Dudley, and acting like a group
of vampiric savages.
And they've got the cheek to be ashamed of me
when I nip into next-door's garden
and sink me fangs into a lovely row of
drumhead cabbages.

Why did I become vegetarian?
Well, it just didn't seem right
ripping the jugular from your friends and family's necks
felt a bit, y'know, funny.
Anyway I've got superhuman strength
and the ability to change into fierce creatures
the poor bastards didn't stand a chance
I was little more than a superhuman bully.
So I made up my mind to
give blood products up altogether
and y' know now I haven't got all that guilt
I'm altogether a much nicer fella.

Don't get me wrong, it's a bit of a struggle
and some smells still drive me wild
like courting couples in the moonlight
or the fresh tender flesh of a newly born child.
We're not all like Bela Lugosi
skulking round graveyards terrorising virgins
don't believe the hype
that's what really pisses me off about Dracula,
Nosferatu and Vlad -
they might think they're fabulous
but politically, they're just perpetuating a stereotype.

Oh it's not easy being the only vegetarian vampire
of old Dudley town
it's far from perfection
for example I never know if me hair looks nice
for me vegetarian functions
'cos I don't cast a bloody reflection.
I'm just feeling sorry for myself now, mustn't grumble
'cos I can always console myself by sucking the juice
from a lovely bowl of rhubarb crumble.

I just potter around now
keep myself to myself
live my undead life quietly
which is just as well really
because between you and me
I'm the only member of the
Dudley Vegetarian Vampire Society.

Kinky Boy

Kinky Boy gonna show you a good time
Kinky Boy gonna make the sun shine
on your spunk stained dirty leather
Kinky Boy gonna be forever printed on your
matt black satin soul
Kinky Boy gonna be the stole you tighten
round your neck
Kinky Boy gonna make us sweat together
hot beads of molten silver
cutting skin like slivers of liquid glass
Kinky Boy gonna spank your ass
red raw honey
gonna make you beg for more
for my hot sweet honey
dripping onto your flesh and red velvet lips and kiss
Aahh
what kisses sugar.

Kinky Boy gonna make you wet with spit
gonna hit you with a second skin of saliva
until we're slippin' n' sliding
in and out of each others fantasy.
Kinky Boy gonna make you dance with me
gonna grind your mind and body into sweet submission
until I'm controlling each incision
and cutting into every inch of
this kinky religion.

Kinky Boy gonna knock, knock, knock
on the door of your soul
Kinky Boy gonna lick any hole you open to me
Kinky Boy gonna be putty in your hands
gonna smile and understand

when you tell me you like being bound and gagged
I'm gonna be the best time you ever had
Kinky Boy gonna be mean
gonna beat you so you gotta bleed
gonna bite the hand that feeds
gonna bring you to your knees
gonna fill your every need.

Kinky Boy a baby
Kinky Boy a lady
Hot ass dominatrix sugar.
Kinky Boy gonna smother you honey
gonna be your mother honey
gonna spend your money honey
on new ways of getting us high.
And why sugar?
'Cos Kinky Boy does what he's told
Kinky Boy knows who holds the purse strings
Kinky Boy thankful for those things.

Drag Is Dead

See the camp man-she
miming like a banshee
wig to stiletto
in lurex and lies
will she won't he
lip sync Shirley Bassey
licking lips
goldfingering thighs
woman hating man-girl
feather boa unfurled
dragnet cast
unrepentantly wide
fish man in fishnets
racist gags and twin sets
all this and more
behind false eyelashed eyes.

Isn't she funny
isn't he a scream
all tits 'n' ass
and strawberry ice-cream
lamé protagonist
filthy mind perverted
finding solace
preaching to the converted
insults another woman
milks another story
sparkling resplendent
in all his fascist glory.

Drag is dead
put it to bed
lay this misogyny to rest.

Hear the sad she-him
play the same act verbatim
up and down the country
from dusk 'til dawn
incessantly hating
unmercifully berating
commercially slating
rejoicefully denigrating
the female form.
Remember ladies, they're deadly serious
when condemning you for having periods.

And in his finale
she will banally
spout more baloney
and if you're lucky
blow a Mae West kiss
to hundreds of thunderous white gay arms applauding
whilst "More, more" they're calling.
What I don't understand is why we tolerate this.

Drag is dead
put it to bed
lay this misogyny to rest.
Drag is dead
put it to bed
lay this misogyny to rest.
Drag is dead
put it to bed
lay this misogyny to rest.

Zip it up in a body bag
R.I.P. Drag.

It's Almost As If Hitler Won
(Muscle Mary Quite Contrary)

A new army
modelled on definition and perfection
the smallest waist
the tightest buns
the longest erection
with cheekbones for weapons
these new clones are steppin' out
turnin' heads, talkin' money
their skin so brown
it must always be sunny on their side of the street
as they stride and compete
man meat tucked neatly in place
aligned to precision
each decision made
by the newest magazine
dictating where to be seen
day dreaming Hollywood, sunshine and profit
the soldiers of this Armani
marches on its wallet.

Credit obsessed
but no credit given to what went before
the history of effeminacy they try to ignore
dilute and keep quiet.
These great men
wouldn't dirty their hands
throwing bricks at the Stonewall riots.

I head for despair when I see what we've done
because sometimes
it's almost as if Hitler won.

Emporium symposium
decorum gymnasium
the new language of the new male order.
Good grief!
There's a world out there
surely that's more important
than any product you can put on your hair.
Will we start to care
about what really matters
before our society crumbles, shatters
and we're left rummaging through the tatters
of vanity and greed?
Why sow such a seed?
I had no idea
our next shared experience
would be the shelving units from Ikea.
There's still so much to be done
the war isn't won
and an army can't march on it's ego.
You can look good
but just let go of your new square jaw.
Must we be so rich
There has to be poor,
be so strong
it isolates the weak?

We can speak for each other
as sister and brother
but only if we can be bothered.

When I see us move toward
this fashion violence so adored
I'm left in silence
so appalled
yet mesmerised

by the body beautiful
it's wonderful curve and line
a place for everything
and everything in its place
such a finely structured face.
Am I staring at the Master race?
When all is said
and all is done
sometimes, just sometimes
it's almost as if Hitler won.

I've Got Hair

I've got hair
it does this
I've got hair
it does this
I've got hair
here
it's eccentric
and sometimes it gets itchy
when I've had sex with dirty strangers

I've got hair
it does this
I've got hair here
it's electric
and sometimes it gets smelly
when I've run out of toilet paper

I've got hair
I've got hair
it's eclectic
like a hunter
like Thor, God of Thunder
but Thor's hair was blonde
not unlike his mother's
she had hair
I'm sure Thor used her Carmen heated rollers.

I've got hair
I've got hair
it's intrinsic
long black
like a high priestess of witchcraft
I'm a mean evil bitch

an evil bitch with hair
shinyblack
like a wet plastic mac brought in from the rain
the mac the lollypop lady wore
she wore with a sou'wester
the sou'wester she wore to keep her hair dry
the lollypop lady's a whore
a whore with thinning hair
which is very noticeable when it's wet
she wants hair
oh, she wants hair
it's quite tragic.

I've got hair
it's not fair
more than my fair share
it's a miracle
like the Virgin Mary
she also had hair
here
that got itchy
when she had sex with dirty strangers.
She loved sex with dirty strangers
because Joseph was homosexual
she would delight in calling him "queerboy"
in front of her friends
He had hair
Oh, he had hair alright
it was permed and streaked
like a common girl's.
Rock Hudson envied him.

I've got hair
I've got hair
it's a freakshow

a kinky afro
like the birth of a million baby spiders
only we don't say coochy coo
because we're scared
spiders make our hair stand on end
in much the same way we make dogs sit and beg
we're pathetic.

Imagine if we didn't have hair
we'd all be shinybright
like candles at a vigil
and if they only took photographs from the sky
then we'd all look the same
except for those who'd been shot in the head.

I've got hair
I've got hair
Ssshhh
it's a conspiracy
I like sex with animals
I sniff glue.

Billy Don't Be An Hairdresser

When Billy was a baby, I knew then
yet I tried to deny the truth
but there was no room for denial
not when Billy's first words were
"Mum, look at the state of your roots!"

I thought it was my fault
wrapping him up in cotton wool
so I tried to toughen him up,
told him to go pot-holing with his Dad
you know, the way mothers do
but he was too busy perming my hair
to play football with the rest of the lads,
he was much happier with a pair of curling tongues
than he ever could be with a snooker cue.

And I said
Billy, don't be an hairdresser
don't be a fool with your life.
Billy, don't be an hairdresser
go out, get yourself a wife.
And as Billy started to grow
I just hung my Purdey Bob low
because Billy did become an hairdresser,
a great big queen.

Now his brother Gavin, he was ever so manly
but he wouldn't let Billy play with him
and it wasn't 'cos he was ashamed, he told me
it's just that every time Gavin sat still
Billy would give his hair a trim.

I remember when he had the measles
and was all spotty and contagious
I went up to his room with a bowl of soup
and he just said
"Get rid of that Purdey Bob, Mum,
you'd look fabulous with a Farah Fawcett-Majors."
I said "Billy, I'm very concerned about you
You act like an effeminate little queer
and it's a tough world out there"
He just looked at me with them sad brown eyes of his
and said "I know Mum,
just think of all those people with really greasy hair."

And I said
Billy, don't be an hairdresser
don't be a fool with your life.
Billy, don't be an hairdresser
go out, get yourself a wife.
And as Billy started to grow
I just hung my Purdey Bob low
because Billy did become an Hairdresser,
a great big queen.

Billy's all grown up now
he owns a chain of salons,
he's done ever so well
and he sees his old mum right and proper
he's always there with a pair of crimpers
if my Purdey Bob comes a cropper.
His profits keep soaring
he opens a new salon every year
and he always says to me with a nod and a wink
"Not bad 'eh Mum,
for an effeminate little queer"

I said "Billy, now you mind your language
'cos I'm very proud, and I'm very, very impressed"
but I do feel sorry for him sometimes
'cos like most hairdressers
Billy's got more hair on his chest
than he has on his head.

And I say, Billy I'm so glad you're an hairdresser
you weren't a fool with your life.
Billy, I'm so glad you're an hairdresser
who needs a bloody wife
(We didn't need your Dad)
and as Billy's empire started to fly
I just held my Purdey Bob high,
'cos Billy did become an hairdresser,
a great big queen.

Faith Is A Toilet

Faith is a toilet
I sometimes piss in
often fondle
occasionally kiss in.

So if you're terribly evangelical
I don't wish to spoil it
but quite simply
for some of us
Faith is a toilet.

I Wanna Be Fucked By Jesus

Forgive me Father for I have sinned.

I wanna be fucked by Jesus
I kiss his statue every day
expecting a kiss back
but his lips are cold
and I'm all alone
and they're the times that I am prone
to these horrible feelings inside
feelings I have to hide
I can only tell Jesus.
He won't let me down
He knows what it's like to suffer
He won't shout or frown upon me
He won't snitch to me family
He just smiles with lips of stone.

I wanna be fucked by Jesus
'cos I love him
and the priest says He loves me
every night I pray
he'll come and stay
and show me what it's like to be
loved by a man
to touch only the way a man can
tell me it's alright
that I'm not alone
but please Jesus, this time
not with lips of stone
but with a mouth soft and gentle.
Kissed by the Lamb of God
"Lamb of God, who takes away the sins of the world
have mercy on us"

I wanna be fucked by Jesus
I see him naked every day
and in so much pain.
When you're hurt that bad
you need someone to love you.
It's not fair
I should be there
I know I could share His agony
and turn it into joy
and it's not just 'cos I'm an altar boy
it's more than that.
I won't say the words for it yet, I can't
but I know Jesus was one too
and I'll tell you why
He didn't want to hurt anybody
nor did he want to fight
deep inside He knows He's right
that the truth will see Him through.
Even me Ma says He loves me
and she never lies.

I wanna be fucked by Jesus
I dream about us naked together
and I get sticky in my underpants
I dream about us naked forever
and I just want the chance
to prove my love is real
to feel Him all over
I want His beard to tickle me face
run His fingers down me chest
and place His hands right there
where no one's ever been before
except the paperboy
but he doesn't count any more
'cos he's not a perfect man who died

to save the world and us from our sins.
And that's where it ends
and that's where it begins.
I say me prayers every night
me eyes closed really tight
hands held together
and praying
I wanna be fucked by Jesus.

Amen.

I Wanna Be Fucked By Jesus Too

Forgive me Father for I have sinned
I'm thinking thoughts I should have binned
it's been twenty-four years since my last confession
but I've got to tell you about my obsession
you see, I want to be fucked by Jesus
and rimmed by the Holy Ghost
I want them to stick
their celestial dicks
right up my heavenly host
I want them to come
right up my bum
and I don't care if you tell my Mum
that I want to be fucked by Jesus!

All God's Children

If devils are the dark side
and roam in the night
then fill my bed with demons
turn on the light.
Let the horny little beasts tease
come over and please me
make sure they squeeze me
with all their might
for I'm no Bo Peep
who's lost her sheep
wandering near and far
I'm no Jack Horner
stuck in the corner
I know exactly where my plums are.

In the privacy of our homes
limited by our screen
the he-she gods reign obscene
thrusting, lusting,
spanking, wanking,
I love it when it hurts
belligerent balls
banging, screaming
fit to burst
bouncing pecs, like eyes on springs
dancing round the torrential spurts.

Eat it, eat it
take it hard
I love your man meat
up my tight arse
come your load and lick my hole.
All God's children got porn in our soul

Who wouldn't love to tussle
with that well oiled muscle
a hustler who could rustle our silk sheets
and then to endeavour
with his throbbing member
fuel the fantasy
of hidden sexual agenda?
Before we're born
we're sworn to hate porn
it's an oath taken in the womb
a solemn mask worn
leaving us forlorn
as we take our denial to the tomb.

I say
Eat it, eat it
take it hard
I love your man meat
up my tight arse.
Come your load and lick my hole
All God's children got porn in our soul.

Let sexuality rule
be led by desire
don't let the puritans douse out your fire.
Set me on fire with petroleum jelly
and throw me belly first through a hoop.
Show me a sauna full of builders
I'll share my problems with the group.
Shit on my face
and make me sing.
If it's good enough for the Pope
then kiss my ring
for I want muscles all over my body
even if they're skinny and spotty

for flesh is flesh whatever the form
sex is sex whatever the norm
so come with me and celebrate
consensual porn.

Eat it, eat it
take it hard
I love your man meat up my tight arse
Come your load and lick my hole
All God's children
All God's children
All God's children got porn in our soul.

We Travel

We travel
alive with sadness and passion
memories charging like stallions
kicking up dust in our battered minds
filled with life
filled with death
fuelled by pride.

We travel alone
with the memories of friends absent but here
each soul still as queer as it was before.
Although we stand baffled we can't ignore
the strength that helps shape our statements
emblazoned sexuality
an insignia on fire as the most sacred of hearts.
We travel hard
like gypsies, tramps and tarts
or soft as summer winds
warm, embracing
still chasing that elusive cure.

We travel
not stagnant still like rancid water
we walk self taught
students of a life even broader than a muscle mary's chest
better than the rest
much more colourful
than the rainbows
faded divas sing about.
We travel
we stomp and shout
there's no stopping us
we're on the move now.

Soldiers of love and sex
marching and mincing on
taking arms
linking up our shared experience
and with bangs bigger than nuclear bombs
the world will hear us
as we travel forward
doors of convention kicked open wide
taking life in our stride
we mustn't hide this depth of feeling
for we're not alone
as we keep reeling.

How can we say goodbye
when memories are a constant reconciliation?
So grab your thoughts and hold them as close
as the loved ones they've replaced
and travel with joy, dignity and celebration.
Don't take no for an answer
you will travel faster
demand a better place
state your destination
but make it real
because the yellow brick road was just a figment
of somebody else's imagination.

The journey of a million miles begins with a single step
and God, we've trod that path before.
Distance promises twists and turns
maybe the next corner might surprise
but real hope lies in strength and union.
We've all something to say
and a million ways of saying it
but even the biggest gob is louder when a thousand mouths cry

"We're on the move now"
with friends, lovers, bedfellows by our side.

We travel
These are our journeys
This is our life.

My Effeminate Bottom

For years they mocked my big girly hair
laughed at my lipstick
insulted my rouge
I made it look like I didn't care
but inside I was broken, battered, bruised.
Their name-calling hurt
but how could I stop 'em?
Then I discovered the power of my effeminate bottom.
So with a giggle, a wiggle and a jaunty little jiggle
I threw back the abuse they hurled
I faced my fear and made it clear
I'm queer, I'm powerful and I can change the world.

So I jumped from my closet
into the most exquisite of clothes
pins in my ears, chains through my nose
my body draped in jewellery and junk
I was Carnaby Street's first gingham punk
So with a stagger, a swagger
and lips like Mick Jagger
I spat, I pogo'd, I swirled
Never mind the bollocks
make mine ten gin and tonics,
Cos I'm queer, I'm powerful and I can change the world.

My effeminate bottom's hot
it's got what it takes to give the best that it's got
covered in loons or peeking through a bikini
it whistles a better Pink Panther than Henry Mancini.
It looks fabulous in funfur
even if the funfur's fake.
It can be as tight as a fist or wider than Victoria Lake.
So mark my words

don't think 'em solemn
one day we will take over the world
with our effeminate bottom.

I've realised I can be free
to do whatever I please
and it pleases me to tantalise and tease
I'm just too good to ever be forgotten
and will always be remembered
for my effeminate bottom.
So with a ding, a dong
the occasional ping pong
a celebratory song in my heart
and my red flag unfurled
I'm safe in the knowledge
that we have the courage
Because we're queer, we're powerful
and we can change the world.

I Don't Have A Cunt

I don't have a cunt
nor too much up front
why even a guide dog can
tell you I'm a man.

I don't have a fanny
I'm like a childless nanny
just take a little poke
it'll prove that I'm a bloke.

I was born with a cock
and as my bollocks ran amok
I realised with a shock
I had to wear this gingham frock.

Am I a contradiction?
Do I deserve conscription?
Why must they all frown
upon me and my gingham gown?

Minority in minority
no-one's priority
I hope against hope
and pray to the Pope
that perhaps Prince Edward might
be a transvestite.

I don't have a beaver
for I'm a firm believer
in taking things as they come
right up my bum.

You may think me base
you might think me tacky
you could be forgiven for thinking
that I'm quite wacky
but fully dressed or in the nude
I'm just a queer with attitude.

Spud-u-Like In Monochrome

I went to the chip shop the other day
in my gingham gown
my lips red, my rouge a browny beige
I asked Mrs Ling for Beef Biryani Fried Rice
half and half
Ha ha ha ha ha
how we laughed
half and half
in the chip shop
clip clop, flip flop, slip slop, tip top
gingham gown.

A man came in
and asked for chips
Great British chips
he stressed with his Nazi voice
and swastika eyes
I stand proud
resplendent in my gingham gown
and scream Fuck off! you nasty Nazi
from the chip shop
clip clop, flip flop, slip slop, tip top
gingham gown.

I went to Ye Olde Patisserie this morning
in my gingham hipsters
the chip shop was shut
so was Pizza Hut
and my feet were covered in blisters.
"You're a different kettle of fish"
said a man with a Pyrex dish
I looked to the ground
and gave a little frown before I struck him down.

Hungry and cold
feeling worn and old
I was drawn to the smell of Spud-u-Like.
It was there I met Theadolite
she was black and I was white
and wore a gingham gown.
Oh ebony and ivory
a mansion house, a priory
Forget Stevie Wonder and Paul McCartney
it's Theadolite and Chloe
piling on the pounds
at Spud-u-Like in town
clip clop, flip flop, slip slop, tip top
gingham gown.

Universal Rentboy (II)

We've been so high
We've touched the sky
We've even watched our best friends die.

Gingham Footnotes

Mirrorballin': a journey into the whirlwind that is the ultimate drugs high - something I've reached on many an occasion. "Rave on, Madchester".

The Queen Sucks Nazi Cock: in light of Prince Philip's recent and constantly recurring racial faux pas, this poem examines the sexual relationships of our Hanoverian heirarchy. "This is no gag."

Licking Prince Charles' Arse: dedicated to the continual betrayal by those so-called Left-wing alternative comics in the early eighties. "How's Andrew Lloyd Webber, Ben?"

Crash! Bang! Wallop! What A Picture!: a brutal tribute to probably the only Royal with a revolutionary heart. "Shame it packed in."

Skinny Wee Dalek: a mythical account of Doctor Who's only companion who was a heroin-addicted Glaswegian dyke. She had her first cigarette in the womb, at sixteen had spent more time in detention centres than Nelson Mandela, and was force fed scotch just to keep her alive. She is Sarah Jane McTuckey. "She's bigger on the inside."

Never Trust A Fella Whose Legs Are Too Close Together: a bleak relook at the sad hipocrisy that surrounded the death of Stephen Milligan, MP, and so-called head sleaze merchant of the decaying Tory years. "Satsumas are not the only fruit."

Mind The Gap: probably the true story of Lucifer's rejection from the banal candyfloss utopia of God's Heaven, as told by the Dark Lord himself. "Thank you, Jamie McCarthy."

Kinky Boy: one rent boy's tale of his universe. There are many others too numerous to count. (Call Chloe - 0898...)

I Wanna Be Fucked by Jesus 1 & Too: an autobiographical account of a twelve year old altar boy from Liverpool, and his love and passion for the Catholic Church's head honcho, followed by subsequent redemption. "I remember Jesus was well-hung on that cross."

All God's Children: as one of life's most prolific voyeurs, this poem is a paean to my ideological desire that is empowering, consensual pornography. "All things are possible."

We Travel: ah, poor Brenda.